Seed Thoughts
for
Christian Prayer
and
Meditation

James J. Stewart

Copyright 2015
James J. Stewart

ISBN: **978-0-9861334-6-6**

Other books by the author:

Gaardian Tales (Christian Fantasy Fiction)
Life Before Conception
Starlight Adventures
The Still Small Voice
Stepping Beyond
The Gaardian Saga [The four above in one volume]

Other Fiction
Casting Lots
Tom's Town

Poetry and Inspiration
Faith and Yosemite [Christian poetry with pictures]
Faith Fuel
Lasting Love
Walking in Faith

Yosemite Picture Books
Ever-Changing Yosemite Valley
Faith and Yosemite [see above]
Portraits of El Capitan
Portraits of Half Dome
Starlight Over Yosemite

Foreword

Sometimes a Christian has a hunger to pray but does not know where to begin. This book can help. Each page contains a statement reflecting the Christian faith in some way. On each page is a starting point, from which the reader's prayers and meditations can begin.

Christian prayers can be formal or casual. They can express a hunger within for help beyond the one praying. They can be simply a desire to connect with greater knowledge, increased power, or larger perspective. Prayer can also be unique for the individual.

You may be at the beginning of your spiritual journey, a spectator who has seen others have an effective prayer life, and you want some of what you have observed in others. You may be a seeker, further along in your faith, and seeking a better, more satisfying prayer life. If you're a student and follower of Jesus, and you have Him in your heart, these seed thoughts may provide fuel for the spiritual fire burning within you. If you have the mature faith of a kingdom-builder, these seed thoughts may kick-start your day.

As these prayer seeds take root, may you have the vision, the faith, and the courage to be the person God created you to be.

~~***~~

Each Christian is part of a large spiritual community. Your successes and failures are part of the successes and failures your community. Your sickness and, ultimately, your death, are a sickness and a death in our part of your spiritual community.

~~***~~

Loving grace and generosity have lasting rewards. As a friend named Tom Elliot once said to me, "You can't take it with you, but you can send it on ahead."

~~***~~

Though God may or may not yet have fulfilled your lifelong dream of marriage and children, you can still struggle to be faithful with the abundance of God.

~~***~~

Jesus tells us that, if we have faith and do not doubt, we will not only do what He did, but even if we say to a mountain, 'Be taken up and thrown into the sea,' it will happen. Today's mountain may be a problem for which you cannot see a solution. Nothing is too difficult for God, however, and He is ready to help with far more than you usually think to ask – including the small stuff.

The Apostle Paul advises followers of Jesus to seek to prophesy. The challenge is not just in the spiritual homework. Quite often, what God gives us to say is met with skepticism or even hostility. Furthermore, as Jeremiah discovered, the response is too often, 'you can't be right.' Still, if God gives you something to say to someone, you can't run away from your responsibility – as Jonah did, and who faced the consequences.

~~***~~

If the Yellowstone caldera becomes a volcano as a few are beginning to fear, how many will die from the ensuing nuclear winter? Will there be environmentalists still insisting that humankind's role in our environment is more important than God's role? There will those who act as though they are wise and wonderful saviors, and who have the perfect agenda for others. Jesus is the only Savior.

~~***~~

Growth and change are often difficult, even painful. Letting go of the past sets you free to thrive in the present. Worse, we sometimes idolize the people and things we have now. When you do this, you hold yourself back from receiving the exciting future and all of its blessings that God has prepared for you.

~~***~~

Followers of Jesus are called to serve Him, and He equips us to serve Him in His way. Jesus is in charge, not those who accept or reject His followers.

~~***~~

David knew he was to be King two decades before Saul died, and David became king. It's a good reminder that you should never give up on a vision God has given you, but to be patient with divine timing.

~~***~~

When Abraham sent his servant to secure a wife for his son Isaac, the servant prayed to his master's God, and God answered his prayer. Each of us becomes a follower of Jesus because another follower -- perhaps more than one -- shared their faith with us. With Jesus in your heart, you have an obligation to pass Him on to others.

~~***~~

It is amazing how our spiritual life can grow, when we start thanking God for His answers to our prayers before we witness those answers. Thanking God in advance for blessings can have an astonishing impact upon your spiritual journey.

~~***~~

When someone is on your mind for no logical reason, pray for them, for they may well be in need of your prayers. When you're praying and your mind wanders to someone or something else, discuss it with God. The Holy Spirit has amazing ways of guiding and moving us. You can trust God with the process – always.

~~***~~

Some spiritual disciplines are more challenging than others. Extensive times in prayer or fasting are examples. Greater effort yields greater rewards. Sunday-only faith is not as satisfying and fulfilling as 24/7 faith. Do you want to thrive?

~~***~~

If faith is not risky, it is not faith. Trusting God with everything and everyone means putting yourself in God's hands. It means focusing on what God wants rather than upon what other people say about you and what you should do.

~~***~~

If we focus upon ourselves, how others see us, and what others think of us, we actually fail to live. We merely exist. If you focus upon caring for others and building them up, you begin to see how much God seeks to bless His children. Acting out of God's love, you fully begin to live and find your fulfillment.

~~***~~

God has been graciously generous toward the people in the United States of America until now. Those denying God in their lives, and those betraying their relationship with Jesus are storing up wrath for themselves. The feel-good television evangelists seldom choose to talk about this.

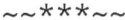

Atheists say there is no God. Some progressives say government is superior to religion, and some religious fanatics say they are doing what God would do if only God had all the facts. Soon enough, God will have His say.

The Lord does everything well and cannot make mistakes. When people not walking their walk with Jesus are blessed, they too often speak of themselves as 'lucky' instead of blessed. Those who know they are blessed enumerate them, and they speak of them with all who will listen. Do you believe in luck, or do you believe in God?

~~***~~

Sometimes what we really want is identical to what we cannot have, and the best thing to do is discuss it with God. Surrendering our dilemma to God brings release for the pressure that may build within us. Prayer helps us put life's paradoxes and mysteries into perspective.

~~***~~

Real joy for a Christian requires a close relationship with Jesus. Any worthwhile relationship takes effort and work as well as time. If your faith seems to be "drip-dry," it is unlikely you have discovered the joy that is possible in really knowing the Lord. The Lord has all kinds of time for you -- do you have time for Him? Is your faith an abridged edition or full-blown?

God gives us all kinds of possibilities for our lives, even when we think our possibilities are limited or our choices poor. It's up to us to make the most of what God gives us. It is up to us to make the most of the life we have. It is up to us to make the most of the relationships God helps us to establish. It's up to us to make the most of the faith we have. It is up to us to make the most out of our whole church. It is up to us!

If you believe, only by faith, that something is about to happen, do you say so? If it is by faith, is it something that God has actually revealed to you? If so, you have to determine through prayer if God wants you to declare what He has revealed, and after that pray that you may be faithful.

~~***~~

God does everything well – God does not make mistakes. There will not be a worldwide flood again, but justice will rain down.

~~***~~

Before God formed us in our mothers' wombs, He knew us and made plans for us. During our spiritual gestation time in these bodies, we're supposed to become mature spiritual beings, in tune with God, ready for heaven. If you're not growing spiritually and becoming more like Jesus, you're merely existing and, eventually, dying.

~~***~~

When Jesus says the pure in heart see God, it's character He's wanting us to grow. Such growth makes pure the path you boldly trod, while living life amid both friends and foes.

~~***~~

Some see their lives as pure, without a care, not thinking if their stance brings others to harm. Without a humble thought, they often dare to act as though beyond God's mighty arm.

~~***~~

When pure in heart, a Christian dares to be a person who fulfills God's plans and more. Without restrictions, God then sets them free to find God's blessings and His joy in store.

~~***~~

Your value is not in y accomplishments, because Jesus determined y value on the cross.

~~***~~

It's easy to blame God when we don't get our way or when things go wrong. There's a better way.

~~***~~

Be thankful that God calls unworthy and unqualified people to serve Him, just as He called a murderer named Moses and a murderer and adulterer to be Israel's second king. Even if you do not fit the agenda of people with whom you work, you're part of God's agenda wherever He calls you to serve Him.

~~***~~

When God spoke to Jesus in John's gospel (12:28-30), some nearby said it thundered. God also speaks in the silence when you are still enough to know that God is God. People who pray mostly only at meals, in perfunctory ways, or in emergencies seem to seldom listen for God in the silence. Let prayer be your lifestyle. Pause to be still and know that God is God. "Listen" to God in the silence.

It is so hard for us to slow down and engage in our communities. We define ourselves too much in terms of what we do. We give to little time and effort towards who we are in the midst of others, being and doing for others.

Have you felt "driven" to pray for someone who is inexplicably on your mind? When younger, some often get on their knees to pray. Later, with arthritis beginning to creep in, they simply pray in whatever way is convenient or comfortable. In any case, God wants us to be His.

~~***~~

More than any other instruction, God reminds us the most often to remember the Sabbath and keep it holy. We accomplish our most and our best with an adequate rest. It is more than good – it is excellent – to be still and know that God is God.

~~***~~

Intelligence is no substitute for wisdom. Wise conclusions will include enough imagination to produce practical results. Be glad that God helps you keep your feet on the ground!

~~***~~

Surrendering to God does not mean giving in or giving up. It means embracing God's patience and kindness. It means choosing to follow the pathway that God prepared for you before He formed you in your mother's womb. God has never given up on you, despite your failures. God has delivered you. You've been given the eyes to see God's glory. Amazing grace!

Few if any gossips and politicians know that Jesus said, [Matthew 12:36-37 (ESV)] "I tell you, on the day of judgment people will give account for every careless word they speak, for by your words you will be justified, and by your words you will be condemned." God always knows the truth.

Jesus said, [John 15:7 (ESV)] "If you abide in me, and my words abide in you, ask whatever you wish, and it will be done for you." Are you living out this promise?

~~***~~

Being still in our hectic world can be a challenge. Even when we're physically still, our minds can be chaotic. In the quiet of early morning, fully rested, it is good – no, excellent – to be still and know the presence and power of God.

~~***~~

Amazingly patient and ready to forgive, when we're ready to do things His way, God also graciously redeems and blesses.

~~***~~

Mark Twain said, "Kindness is the language which the deaf can hear and the blind can see." When we try to be like Jesus, even the blind and deaf notice us.

~~***~~

Those who claim to follow Jesus but have no mercy, compassion, and joy are living a lie.

~~***~~

There is nothing too difficult for God. He can fulfill the most outrageous dreams He gives us.

~~***~~

When we make our things, pleasure, & power into our gods, the Creator is jealous of us. When we follow Jesus, He is zealous for us.

~~***~~

We can be very rich and not thrive. We can thrive without being rich. God wants us to thrive in Him, bearing His fruit.

~~***~~

The most tempting evils are subtle, apparently harmless. We thrive, and our spirits grow, when we avoid those small temptations.

~~***~~

According to Paul [2 Cor. 1:20] All the promises of God find their "Yes" in Jesus. As we strive to be like Jesus, the promises of God can be fulfilled in us.

~~***~~

The very essence of God is love, so love cannot be a momentary surge of emotion or something that diminishes with time. Love is not something we feel but something we do. God made us so that love is part of who we are, so we can share it with others. Love does not flow in gushing rivers that diminish in dry seasons, but flows from springs that are steady and dependable.

Overwhelmed by all of life's "stuff," if we focus away from it, seeking God first, it's worth the effort.

We need to be able to laugh with children and see happiness dancing in their eyes even while we're struggling against hell. We need balance!

Forgiveness is the flower's fragrance given to the heel that crushed it. Not forgiving is like taking poison & waiting for the other person to die.

~~***~~

Fans of Jesus possess merely a plastic version. Followers have a living Jesus in their hearts, who's transforming them with His power.

~~***~~

For some, this day was the first, and for some, the last. Tomorrow's a day of laughter, or of tears. Each is God's gift, wrapped in expectations.

~~***~~

Walking by faith instead of by sight is for those who have been set free by Christ's crucifixion, His burial, and His resurrection. It is true freedom.

~~***~~

Do you remember the dream God gave you as a child? Pursue it His way instead of your way, and you will see it fulfilled gloriously.

~~***~~

Seemingly little things can poison a relationship. One man's greed disabled God's people after they conquered Jericho. Discipline is vital.

~~***~~

God knows your past and holds your future. Followers of Jesus serve Him today and are blessed through His glory.

~~***~~

Our coinage says, "In God we trust." So should your heart, and your voice.

~~***~~

It's easy to be enslaved to the past. Jesus is the bondage breaker. For true freedom, Christ has set you free.

~~***~~

Before God formed you in your mothers' womb, He knew you and made plans for you. God is patient and kind. His love never fails.

~~***~~

Sometimes God gives dreams that challenge us to greater trust: To see such dreams fulfilled requires those of faith to ask. Have you asked?

~~***~~

Vision isn't limited to things we can see. New beginnings have a path. If the dream has come from God, fulfillment's meant to be.

~~***~~

Using racism as a political talking point is insulting to those who suffer real racism. Accusing others of sin does not render us pure. The book of James says we should bridle our tongues.

~~***~~

The fear of God is the beginning of wisdom. Being in awe of God truly means emotional and spiritual strength in our walk with Jesus.

~~***~~

When we turn towards God's ways, we're forgiven & refreshed by His presence & power through Jesus Christ. Such change is always worthwhile.

~~***~~

God is patient & kind. God has not given up on us no matter how much or how often we go astray. He sent His Son Jesus to die for us, proving His love.

~~***~~

Love does not insist on its own way. God's plans for us made before we were born are fulfilled, but only if we are willing to let God be God.

~~***~~

For mere fans of Jesus, grace is a concept. Fully functional Christians following Jesus dare to be confident in God's grace, staking their lives on it. Are you a fan or a follower?

~~***~~

Nothing is too difficult for God. You can look forward to seeing His handiwork in the future. God does all well.

~~***~~

Do you want a temporary artificial Jesus, who fits your agenda, or do you want the real Jesus that you follow from here into eternity?

~~***~~

As He helps you thrive professionally and personally, let Jesus dwell within your heart, and ask Him to give you strength and wisdom.

~~***~~

Why are so many things described as awesome? I'm in awe of God. Nothing and no one else measures up to being truly awesome. Wise up, world!

~~***~~

When God puts a word on your lips or a task to do, some responses will be receptive & encouraging, but many will not be. Be determined and serve God, not necessarily others.

~~***~~

"Before I formed you in your mother's womb, I knew you and consecrated you," says the Lord. Are you following His path or your own?

~~***~~

When life seems like hell, prayer brings a touch of heaven. So long as we pray, & keep on keeping on, the Lord has work for us to do.

~~***~~

Vainglory or "empty glory" is a subtle, destructive sin arising out of self-worship. It keeps us from thriving. The antidote is humility. This means not thinking less of yourself, but rather thinking of yourself less.

~~***~~

If you're looking for a miracle today, try seeing things through God's eyes. Today's a gift, wrapped in expectancy.

~~***~~

Our prayers for things both big and small are easy to be asked, yet thanks are often not expressed. Sowing of faith's seed begins with giving thanks.

~~***~~

We're often tempted to make decisions without praying first. Being fully surrendered to doing things God's way is not always easy.

~~***~~

We are surrounded by a great cloud of witnesses, who have graduated and gone to heaven. Let's run with endurance the race that is set before us, giving Christ the glory.

~~***~~

Getting someone's trust is an investment you make. Breaking someone's trust is a costly mistake. Do you need forgiveness from someone?

~~***~~

God has prepared someone for you, and He has prepared you for that person. Secure that choice for bountiful blessings, if you have not done so already, and praise God. God does all well.

~~***~~

Current problems prepare you for great glory to come if you keep your focus on God's eternity.

~~***~~

Following Jesus, you can live courageously and cheerfully, despite difficulties, if you trust in what you don't see yet. Do you trust Jesus?

~~***~~

There's joy in heaven when you place your trust in God and then take a leap of faith.

~~***~~

Prayer is essential to your partnership with Christ. You are one in His Spirit, for His love binds you to Him and others. Praise God!

~~***~~

Let go of your worries, and pray for your community. Quietly, meet Jesus, your shepherd, and worship Him. He has already given His life for you. Can you give yourself to Him?

~~***~~

When you removed the price tag on a gift for someone, did you consider the price Jesus paid for your soul?

~~***~~

The key to getting what you need is surrender to God's will, who will always graciously supply your needs. Do you need all you want?

~~***~~

Jesus tells his followers to ask, so ask in terms of His will and His kingdom, and then trust in His process.

~~***~~

Jesus tells his followers to seek, so seek the fulfillment of His plans for your life in His kingdom.

~~***~~

Santa Claus never died for anybody. The cross & empty tomb are close to the manger. Where are you?

~~***~~

The best Christmas gift for God is to give Him all that you are, because He gave us His Son's life that we may live in Him.

~~***~~

Love does not insist on its own way, but if you choose to follow Jesus, you get the blessings on His way.

~~***~~

God's timing is perfect. There's never been a more flawless time to follow Jesus. Yesterday is merely history. Praise God!

~~***~~

God's timing is perfect. His blessings come at the perfect time, not necessarily when YOU want them. Thank God!

~~***~~

Those who talk the talk were in church for Christmas, but those who walk the walk will also serve Him daily.

~~***~~

You have an upward call in Christ Jesus. Neither Santa nor the Easter bunny died for you. Do you seek your calling each day?

~~***~~

Do you have the eyes to see God's will, and do you have the ears to hear His still small voice as He leads you into something new? Seek the courage to know that with God, all things are possible.

~~***~~

In Gethsemane, Jesus surrendered with hope, trusting Our Father. No matter what you face, followers of Jesus do the same. It's His way.

~~***~~

If you're willing to risk everything for the cause of Christ, what you gain will endure forever.

~~***~~

God has equipped you to accomplish far more than you ask or think. It is simply a matter of being on the path divinely prepared for you.

~~***~~

Love is not pushy. No matter how much you love someone, mutual living means mutual decisions, letting go of pride. Are you doing this?

~~***~~

When someone falsely accuses you of something, pray that God will be merciful and gracious towards them. Then forgive them. It's hard, but is Jesus' way.

~~***~~

Your values and God's are different. To see others through God's eyes requires "praytience" -- prayer coupled with patience.

~~***~~

Possibilities are limitless if we approach the Bible with honest humble questions and willingness to change and do things God's way.

~~***~~

When God is revealing a new pathway to you, He's prepared it for you. If pursued, God will multiply your life's success even in the midst of scorn.

~~***~~

Jesus says we'll all be held accountable for every word we utter. I'm paying attention. You?

~~***~~

Do you live a life of Christ-centered love, joy, peace, patience, kindness, goodness, faithfulness, gentleness, and self-control?

~~***~~

John says, "God is love." Paul says, "Love does not insist on its own way." God does not insist on His own way but blesses us when we do things His way.

~~***~~

As Jesus' followers, we are called to serve Him. He's equipped us to serve Him His way. He's in charge, not the critics on the sidelines.

~~***~~

It's great to begin prayer focused on praise & enjoying God's presence and power. Making no requests until fully surrendered is an amazing experience.

~~***~~

If you want God's blessings in your life, you must begin each day wanting God. If you want to take advantage of God's blessings, you must be seeking them. In the end, it will not be the number of your days that counts, but how those days have been fulfilled.

~~***~~

Christians who step out in faith with Jesus discover what Christ can do in their lives. Once we know what is important to us, we have the freedom walk away from the things that aren't really important.

~~***~~

Each of us has our own way of handling bad news. We eventually have to deal with our feelings. We know that Jesus will understand because he was as fully human as we are. We know that whether we are right or wrong, Jesus understands us. God loves a humble and penitent heart. God is most wondrous in the power to redeem us when we let go to God, letting God by God's grace extends us His power and love.

"It is a common experience that a problem difficult at night is resolved in the morning after the committee of sleep has worked on it."
 -- John Steinbeck

~~***~~

~~***~~

Let Jesus finish what He has started in you. His love is eternal and unconditional — don't give up on Him. He hasn't given up on you.

~~***~~

A healthy relationship with God means being as patient with God as God is patient with you. It is true of all relationships.

~~***~~

Since the very essence of God is love, then love cannot be a momentary surge of emotion that diminishes over time. Love is not something we feel but something we do. The shores of a reservoir of love are secured by liking, loving, and trusting. A real reservoir of love is surrounded by mountains and hills of trust, not easily moved, giving security to the relationship.

~~***~~

Jesus is your hope. He will fulfill your life completely as He uses you for His glory. He is your way to everlasting life.

~~***~~

God values submission over success. God graciously blesses those who let Jesus take over their lives. In Christ, you are truly free.

~~***~~

Do you treat God like a cosmic flight attendant, ready to serve you when you press the prayer button above life's passenger seat? Do you want to be in control, able to take credit for the outcome of your prayers? Do you place limits on what you want God to do?

~~***~~

Today, if all for Jesus, will be exciting and exhilarating and exhausting and fulfilling. Praise God!

~~***~~

Happiness is not consumed, earned, or owned as a destination. It is living out God's grace with gratitude.

~~***~~

When you share your faith with someone who already has a personal relationship with Jesus Christ, sharing the faith encourages them and strengthens their faith. A large percentage of our population, however, has never been inside a church. All people are your neighbors, according to Jesus, and all need patience, kindness, forgiveness, an encouraging word, and the saving grace of God in Jesus Christ.

~~***~~

Before God formed you in your mothers' womb, He knew you and had plans for you. God graciously gives us the freedom to go His way and follow Jesus in this life and on into heaven, or we can go our own way.

~~***~~

There is power and truth found only in Jesus. He is the way, the truth, and the life, leading to life eternal.

~~***~~

Praise God for all that He reveals and more: God is faithful to fulfill and help you thrive.

~~***~~

Through your relationship with Jesus, you can use prayer to connect with God's presence and power on His terms.

~~***~~

It is easy to pray as if you are giving orders to God. Far more power is released in our lives, however, when you pray for others than when you pray for yourself. Do you really trust God to do what is best? Real power is unleashed when you surrender totally to God's will. When you let God be God and let Christ be your King, miracles can occur.

~~***~~

The Coast Guard motto is, "We are required to go out, but we are not required to come back." Christians cannot settle for simply experiencing God. You need to share the experience with others. You cannot simply sit and soak. Move on into the mission.

~~***~~

Science would have us limit our understanding of love to the sexual or social chemistry between people. Jesus defines love as much more.

~~***~~

Media editors would limit our understanding of beauty to outward appearances, however those appearances may be altered or enhanced by makeup or plastic surgery. Being photogenic is not the same as being beautiful. God defines beauty, not make-up.

~~***~~

Pundits would limit our understanding of honor to paying our dues only when we get caught doing something inappropriate or unlawful rather than as a record of overall behavior. Honor is much more.

~~***~~

Early church disciples made decisions after worship & fasting, getting the guidance & power of the Holy Spirit. Do you fast or pray before making an important decision?

~~***~~

For most, it is easier to see the focus of God's love in the manger than on the cross, easier to share the joy of the shepherds than the joy of the disciples at Easter, easier to comprehend the reverence of the wise men than the astonishment of those who saw the risen Christ. Is this true for you?

~~***~~

It is better to serve Jesus faithfully, but with difficulty, than to agree with the agenda of another with ease.

~~***~~

Do you consider extensive worship and fasting as a prelude to making an important decision?

~~***~~

God grants you the vision to perceive, faith to believe, & courage to trust in God's ability to achieve His dreams for your life. Thank God!

~~***~~

With awareness of Jesus seeing things through your eyes, you can begin to see things as He does.

~~***~~

Your spiritual vitality depends upon seeing through Christ's eyes and His larger perspective.

~~***~~

At this point in your life, daily routine is like spiritual sandpaper: smoothing rough edges, polishing known expanses. Reading the Bible every day can seem a "chore," perhaps, but you can be better prepared for what lies ahead.

~~***~~

You have both gifts and limitations. Some gifts are obvious. Some of your limitations are obvious. Good stewardship means making the most of your gifts. Good sense means knowing when not to challenge your limitations.

~~***~~

Do you keep your holiness at a distance? Do you want rigid standards for others and mercy for yourself? Few want a preacher as a neighbor.

~~***~~

If you fail to plan, you plan to fail. When Jesus sent out the seventy disciples to do ministry in His name, He told them what to take with them as well as what to do and say. He helped them plan ahead for what they faced. Walk that path.

~~***~~

You can laugh at those who behave like fools, until you remember that part of your calling is to be willing to be a fool for the sake of Christ.

~~***~~

Jesus gives His followers two imperatives: To love one another, and to carry the good news into our sin-filled world. Both commands involve risk. Some people are more difficult to love than others, and the world is not always ready to hear the good news. Still, you have your marching orders.

~~***~~

There is always the temptation to bring Jesus down to your level instead of trying to grow to his level.

~~***~~

Saying you believe in God, and saying you have Jesus dwelling in their heart, are two entirely different things. Either you have heard His call and are seeking Him with your whole heart – or not.

~~***~~

Are you a waterfall of faith words without a drop of common sense, or do you speak the truth about Jesus quietly and listen to others?

~~***~~

You can become vain when comparing yourself with others and easily then become self-destructive. God's love is enough to heal you.

~~***~~

God wants you to get pleasure from your successes as well as your ideas, and to use the gifts He's given you to thrive. Praise God!

~~***~~

Wisdom doesn't come from your education. Ask God for wisdom so you can learn to handle your doubts, your restrictions, and your ignorance with grace and faith.

~~***~~

How has God gifted you to thrive? What is God asking of you? The answers are not found within yourself but through prayer.

~~***~~

No matter how your life is broken, "Lord have mercy," is your prayer for another chance. God's positive answer is ready if you seek Him.

~~***~~

God can accomplish more through you in one day, than you can do for yourself in a thousand years. Let God be God!

~~***~~

God is eternal – He cannot forget anything. To God, your childhood prayers were a moment ago, and those answers can now come decades later.

~~***~~

You can ask for anything in Jesus' name, in His will & purpose, & it will be done. It's a matter of the Holy Spirit's guidance & power.

~~***~~

If you expect God to answer your prayers, it makes sense to be humbly prepared and thankful to receive His blessings.

~~***~~

When sharing your faith, remember: People do not want to endure sound teaching, but having itching ears they accumulate for themselves teachers to suit their own likings.

~~***~~

When you're out of ideas and resources, and you truly and fully surrender to God, that's when divine power is unleashed.

~~***~~

If you have Jesus in your heart, you have a fresh start each day. The past is past, the future is full of hope, and today is an opportunity, a gift.

~~***~~

Wearing the label 'Christian' without mercy, compassion, grace, or joy, is hypocritical. Wannabes can't cut it. Real followers of Jesus do. Do you wear the label appropriately?

~~***~~

Prayer is a team activity where God is the Captain. Praying according to His will, His power is unleashed, and He's glorified.

~~***~~

Honest, humble, and bold prayer transforms the one praying and sets loose spiritual power. If utilized, it works.

~~***~~

Do not feign affection. In the midst of barrenness and disappointments real love endures, even when illogical. Do you follow Jesus' example?

~~***~~

It is easier to look within and pursue what you desire, than to ask what life needs of you and triumphantly answer. What is God calling you to do?

~~***~~

Your life is filled with beginnings and with goals. In between are pain, toil, and struggle. All of it is part of growing towards fulfillment. Recognizing and pursuing God's presence in the midst of it all brings joy.

~~***~~

It is easy to make decisions based upon what is right in our own eyes. Jesus says there is a better way -- to base our decisions upon God's will, rather than upon our own consciences.

~~***~~

Any time you're sneaky, you thumb our nose at Jesus. His actions and teachings instruct you to be honest and straightforward.

~~***~~

Few doubt that Jesus is the greatest intellect in history. He takes great ideas and huge tasks and makes them manageable. Consult with Him!

~~***~~

There is a close relationship between prayer and patience. Practice praytience!

~~***~~

If you insist that everything remains the same and don't trust new ideas and possibilities, you have given up your freedom. When you allow yourself to have alternatives, you are free, but you have to be willing to take risks. Christians need to be ready to be a fool for Christ, to get involved, to be real, and to love unconditionally.

When God sends disaster to the U.S., politicians will blame one another, and voters will claim they didn't vote for them. Can you humble yourself before God with total honesty?

Some expressions are worth comparing.

For the love of God!	For my love for God!
For the love of Christ!	For my love for Jesus!
God so loved the world .	I so love my Lord . . . .

. .	
Jesus loves me, this I know.	I love Jesus, this I know.
Jesus gave his all for me.	I'll give Jesus my all for Jesus.

~~***~~

Worship is expressing one's devotion to God directly to God. You can worship without music but not without prayer. In the fullest sense, worship is not a spectator sport!

~~***~~

Jesus loved and worked with Judas until the end. Up through the day before the betrayal, Jesus was patiently teaching Judas along with the others. Have you ever betrayed your faith in Jesus?

~~***~~

You can't refocus your inner desires and emotions without God's help, but Christ within you can make everything fresh and new.

~~***~~

Don't make excuses for yourself or for others, but be humbly accepting. You may not like what others do, but you can be compassionate. That is the Christian way.

~~***~~

As a Christian, you are challenged to sacrifice your personal goals and commitments for the sake of Christ. Do you?

~~***~~

Paul says, "For freedom, Christ has set us free" (Galatians 5:1). If you're enslaved to your passions or addictions, you're not free, but Jesus is ready to help.

~~***~~

Are you dreaming the impossible dreams of the future, living in the rosy past, or doing the Christ-faith work of the present?

~~***~~

God loves a humble penitent heart. God graciously redeems you when you surrender to God's holy power and love.

~~***~~

A painful truth spoken can spoil a beautiful friendship, unless both people love unconditionally as Jesus teaches us to do. Do you need to reconcile with someone or with God?

~~***~~

You can avoid suffering & sorrow for a time, but you take risks in order to learn, feel, change, grow, & love -- & truly live. God can help.

~~***~~

Authentic praying is dangerous business, but the rewards can be beyond your wildest dreams. Be both honest and humble.

~~***~~

With Christ's peace, shalom, within you, chaos around you matters less. Just be still and know that God is God.

~~***~~

Letting go of your pride and turning control over to God appears to be very risky business, but "No guts no glory!"

~~***~~

Walking in your wilderness, remember that God makes all things new. There are yet new things to see and hear.

~~***~~

God's will is set before you if you have the eyes to see and the ears to hear. It is a matter of your stepping out in faith.

~~***~~

Friendships seem to unravel when Christians say, "Do it my way" to each other, rather than serve one another in the name of Jesus. Have you been too forceful with anyone?

~~***~~

Living the life of a Christian means you must also work that life. Being must include doing, or else your faith is incomplete.

~~****~~

The cross that some wear is a proclamation of faith, but it's not enough. Symbols are useful if they aren't just decorations. It's better to +be+ a symbol of faith in Christ. Are you a symbol of Christ and His love?

~~****~~

Faith is the substance of things hoped for, but that substance cannot be detected, weighed, or measured scientifically. Faith is the evidence of things unseen, but such evidence is not admissible in the court of common logic. If your faith appears foolish, so what? Authentic Christians can be fools for the sake of Christ.

~~****~~

God speaks to you through music - even when the music doesn't have words. The Holy Spirit makes itself known to you through the music in your soul. Sometimes finding the power of the Holy Spirit is simply a matter you of letting out the music within you.

~~****~~

Faith is a living and growing thing, and your faith needs a framework just as surely as your flesh needs a skeleton to give it shape. Prayer can be a lifestyle.

~~****~~

Spiritual disciplines provide direction to your Christian faith when it is floundering. Having direction can help you focus, dealing with your challenges creatively.

~~****~~

Spiritual disciplines provide strength when you are weary of things that won't resolve. They toughen the muscles of our Christian faith.

~~***~~

Spiritual discipline creates appreciation for the gifts that God has given you. Study and prayer help you discover gifts and strengths you never knew God had given you. Discipline means work, but you can find that the results far exceed your expectations or your input simply because God is God, and Christ is King.

~~***~~

It is natural to want to be your own boss. Your calling, however, is to be like Jesus, and set your mind on things of the Spirit. It is the path to holiness.

~~***~~

The only way for you to trust God is to take risks, believing the results are always in your best interest. People of little faith will accuse you of being naive. Which is more important - your image with your friends or your relationship with your God?

~~***~~

Jesus teaches us to love one another equally. We are fully equal, with the empty tomb the greatest equalizer of all.

~~***~~

When you say, "I don't care," you deny Jesus' call to love. If you say, "It doesn't matter to me," when your help is needed, you are betraying your faith. You are "called" to care, to be involved, to be concerned, to love, to shun apathy, and to shun procrastination. Your response to that call to love is crucial to your faith.

~~***~~

What if you had grown up in Nazareth two thousand years ago? Would you have noticed the Christ child in your neighborhood? What is God doing right now that you are not noticing?

~~***~~

Jesus invites you to walk on water with Him. Yes, you cannot risk without possibility of failure, but you are called to step out in faith and get out of the boat! The other eleven did not even try to get out of the boat. At least, Peter tried!

~~***~~

Jesus risked it all for your sake. To be His follower means caring enough to risk it all for His sake. It may merely mean sacrificing the status quo, but it may also mean risking the loss of everything. Do you dare? Can you do less?

~~***~~

If you're totally satisfied with how you see yourself and your world, don't ask Jesus into your heart. Your life will be transformed if you do.

~~***~~

To be Christ-centered is more important than just appearing like you are. True abundance can only be found in your heart when it is centered on Jesus.

~~***~~

Physical fitness without emotional and spiritual fitness is almost pointless. Did you have dreams of being an athlete? In the real world, you have the physical, emotional, and spiritual tools to be able to enjoy the abundant life that God has provided. Thank the Lord!

~~***~~

There's no evidence that Jeremiah questioned his effectiveness as a pastor and prophet when God's people didn't listen to him.

~~***~~

In these troubled times, all the church has a great need for people like Barnabas. Let's not insist on our own way but rather be "children of encouragement."

~~***~~

It helps a marriage for each partner to say they love each other, and the same is true for a relationship with God. You may have sung of Jesus being your friend, but have you ever done something because you wanted to be Jesus' friend?

~~***~~

Joy is being glad that we are alive, putting our regrets behind us and our hopes in front of us. Joy is a thundershower in the center of a heat wave, warm sunshine in the midst of winter. It is found in Fall colors, Spring blossoms, painted deserts, and clear mountain lakes. Joy is finding the King of Kings in a manger and not finding him in a tomb.

When we've lived in the same place for a long time, do we remember to be as thankful for that home after time has passed -- as thank full as we were at the beginning? How often do we express our thanks to friends for their friendship? How often do we thank God for God's loving kindness? How often do we tell our families what they mean to us? How often, other than on Sunday, do we praise God for the gift of God's Son, Jesus Christ?

Evangelism means sowing the seed of the Good News (inviting), so that the church can water (welcome), so that in turn God will bring a harvest (growth in spirit and ministry).

~~***~~

Most of us hold up equality as an ideal, quoting the Declaration of Independence. Very few truly believe we are the equals of our neighbors. If we realize we can find grounds of equality with every human being, God's peace would be a reality bringing order to our chaotic world.

~~***~~

One of life's real pleasures for me is being able to worship without being preoccupied with the mechanics of what's going on. I love it when people are as excited about worship as I am! I am glad that our praise team plays together with the congregation in a "family" spirit. Amazing things happen when we are all willing to let God be God and let Christ be King.

~~***~~

A poem by Robert Frost named "Fire and Ice" says:
"Some say the world will end in fire,
Some say in ice.
From what I've tasted of desire
I hold with those who favor fire.
But if it had to perish twice,
I think I know enough of hate
To say that for destruction ice
Is also great And would suffice."
Many people believe that "the end" is near. Jesus teaches that such "signs" are irrelevant.

~~***~~

Are we expressionless saints who stare out at the world and don't get involved, or are we the brash children of God, ready to tackle anything?

~~***~~

Jesus teaches unconditional love as both possible and rewarding. Christian love is a response to the call of Christ. His authentic followers choose to love as He does.

~~***~~

William Blake said, "What is now proved was once only imagined." The future of the church depends upon our tapping into the imagination of Christ. It is His church! Our eternity is in His hands!

~~***~~

Music is a great vehicle for approaching God. Worship is the road, and our destination is eternal.

~~***~~

Jesus Christ is the window through whom we see God. The closer we get to the window, the more we see of God.

I sometimes hear from people about their hopes, less often about what God hopes for them. It is an awesome responsibility to speak on behalf of God's dreams, for no sane person wants to be a false prophet. Let's pursue God's dreams!

~~***~~

As a Christian, does your life reflect the fact you've said yes to Jesus? Which of your gifts are being used by His church? What is He asking of you?

~~***~~

God does not ask you to do anything without first equipping you for the job. Consequently, one of the best ways to determine God's will for yourself is to examine the gifts that you have been given.

~~***~~

Fear of punishment tends to teach appropriate behavior. Fear of shame induces honorable behavior. In your efforts to express God's love, don't lose your moral compass.

~~***~~

The fear of God puts other fears into perspective, then God's love can cast out all of your fears.

~~***~~

God is often the initiator of prayer. Christians continue to stand apart from (as well as within) society when we respond to the call within us. Do you satisfy your hunger for the eternal? Are you a fully functional Christian? Are you an integral part of Christ's church?

~~***~~

"Take delight in the LORD, and he will give you the desires of your heart," said King David.

~~***~~

Conclusions are based on both facts and assumptions. Assuming God wants what is best for you, and assuming God has the power to achieve that best, your conclusion can naturally be to trust.

~~***~~

God told Moses to write down starting points, stage by stage. As a Christian, are you starting anything today for God? What's the current stage of your journey with Jesus?

~~***~~

The joy of Jesus is a Christian's strength. You can lose much of your zest because you do not allow yourself the joy that He wants for you. When you have a party, Jesus wants to be there!

~~***~~

It is relatively easy to offer answers people don't ask for. It is much harder to set the tone that leads people to ask questions about Jesus. Each Christian must set the tone, so that unchurched people can see Christ is at work in us.

~~***~~

Each day you have lots of familiar things to do. You also have opportunities for new things to try. Each day is a gift wrapped in the tissues of expectancy. You can fill the day with love, hope, peace, faith, and joy.

~~***~~

To discover God's dreams for your life you spend time in conversation with God's Son. That conversation should involve at least as much listening and meditation as it does talking. God gave you two ears and one mouth. Listen for His still small voice.

~~***~~

Faith in God means more than trusting in God's ability to achieve God's will and our dreams. Faith is trusting God enough to know that God will do it.

~~***~~

The vast majority of all church members became part of the church because someone invited them or brought them.

~~***~~

Most Christians routinely count our obvious blessings - for material possessions, for friends, for loved ones, for life, for health, for home, and for family. When we read the Book of Psalms, they do not so much thank God for what has been delivered to them, but rather they thank God for that from which God has delivered them.

~~***~~

While we cannot see things through God's eyes, what we can do is recognize how we relate to a God who sees things differently than we do.

~~***~~

Love does not give up hope even when the other person seems hopeless. The loving person hopes for, waits for, and expects the best from the one loved. When you love someone, you desire the best for them and in them.

~~***~~

Enduring a crisis often means letting go of your control, bearing all things (including your ego) and turning it all over to Jesus Christ.

~~***~~

Real love does not come from within us. It comes from God. We are merely a channel/valve through which that love flows.

~~***~~

The Chinese have an old proverb. "Absence is to love what wind is to fire -- it extinguishes the small and enkindles the great." Real love, the love that flows from God through us to others, has God's greatness.

~~****~~

Are you determined to fulfill God's dream for you, willing to put the fulfillment of this dream ahead of literally everything else in your life? If you don't have the time and energy, it's not from God.

~~****~~

God does not require that we be perfect, or that we achieve perfection on the first try, for God keeps on redeeming us - and redeeming our mistakes. God does want us to keep on growing.

~~****~~

To love unconditionally involves risks. While conditional love helps feed our own egos, unconditional love nurtures our relationship with Jesus Christ.

~~***~~

A challenge from Jesus is, "Take the risk and let yourself be defined in terms of what you are for, and in terms of who you love. No matter what, I am always with you!"

~~***~~

Is your life as confident and Christ-centered as it could be? Are you as assertive as you could be in witnessing to what you believe in? You would be surprised at the difference it will make for your life.

~~***~~

Jesus showed us how we, the creatures, can be more like the creator. You have to keep on trying to learn to be like Him. It's the education of a lifetime!

~~***~~

Ponder the situations from which you have been delivered, and the people from whom your life has been delivered. Ponder the resulting life that has been delivered to you, both in days past and in the present. Ponder the hopes and dreams that are yours because God is a deliverer, His promises are repeatedly fulfilled, and how He is so amazingly gracious. Ponder what you hope will be delivered and your sense of peace as you wait, because you know that God's way will be the best way even if it is not your way.

~~***~~

Why not do your best with your responsibilities, let others do their best with their responsibilities, love one another enough to trust one another, love God enough to trust God, and then let God be God and let Christ be King?

~~***~~

Will you at the end of your day, be able to say, "I walked today where Jesus walked?" Do you begin your day by inviting the companionship of Jesus for the day? When you go to a party, do you invite Him along?

~~***~~

It has been proven countless times that people who read their Bibles daily live healthier and happier lives. It is the best therapy around in terms of preventative medicine - physically, mentally, spiritually.

~~***~~

Good stewards make the most of the gifts God has given them, and by so doing they are an effective witness to God's limitless love and grace. Are you a good steward?

~~***~~

Just as surely as we know the good news of the Christian faith, we also need to live the good news and spread this news that is too good to keep.

~~***~~

Even the telephone is an instrument of ministry. Encouragement is a ministry. Prayer is a ministry. It is all a matter of caring.

~~***~~

Easter Monday is known as The Day of Holy Laughter. It is a day for having good clean fun and telling jokes because we are celebrating how God had the last laugh on the Devil when Christ arose from the grave.

~~***~~

Open your ears and eyes to all the ways God chooses to be revealed to you. It may mean silencing our own voice and those around you long enough to hear what God has to say. The Voice did say to the Psalmist, "Be still and know that I am God!"

~~***~~

Like God, you have to be ready to forgive. You have to be ready to acknowledge that everyone makes mistakes. We are all sinners. In the Christian sense, we must be ready to return to Jesus the love he showed for us. After all, he died for our sins that we might be forgiven.

~~***~~

Jesus seems to say the abundant life is more accessible to the poor than to the rich! Count your blessings instead of pennies. Since the Lord is supplying your every need, that is the essence of the abundant life that Jesus talks about.

~~***~~

Pray for those who are sick, so they may be healed and returned to active duty in the Christian community. Pray for those who for any reason choose not to worship with the rest of the community, that they may be tuned into the guidance and power of the Holy Spirit.

~~***~~

If you begin your day with communing with God, you won't have to race down the freeway. If you are at peace with yourself, you won't feel compelled to respond to the nervous chatter of everyone you meet. Empowered by God, you can actually enjoy an elevator ride. When you properly begin your day, your mind is so organized you need not be late for anything.

The people who design software are called programmers. The greatest programmer who ever lived is Jesus Christ. If we allow Jesus to "program" our minds, we can live the fullest and most satisfying life that is possible -- the Christian life. Are you letting Jesus "program" your own personal software?

Living the Christian life so you actually love your neighbors as yourself means you have to decide regularly to love. You decide to be patient and kind, not to be jealous or boastful, not to be arrogant or rude. The challenge is to continue deciding to love even when that love is not returned.

~~***~~

Life can be an adventure in faith. It can be a time of your taking delight in all that God has provided and is providing. Life itself is a miracle, and your relationship to God opens your eyes to miracles all around you. Your Christian eyes are open to the greatest miracle of all: Christ's empty tomb!

~~***~~

"The Lord moves in mysterious ways" can be said if you are willing to spend a lifetime studying God's movements and God's will. "The Lord moves in mysterious ways" can also be said if you simply love to bask in the warm presence of God. You allow yourself to be filled with wonder, awe, and peace.

Face to face, you can tell Jesus you have received His gift, thank Him for it, and offer yourself in return. You are the only thing that is really yours to give in return. If you give yourself, then Christmas is yours forever.

Scripture has a cleansing power for your mind. When you are tense and irritable, reading scripture helps clear away the debris of the day's events.

~~***~~

Jesus is not a beautiful balloon drifting in and out of your life. Jesus is a person of substance who, as your constant companion, is your ultimate friend. You can always depend upon him.

~~***~~

God gives you all that you need, including the gift of His presence and power in any situation that comes your way. God is for you, so who (or what) can be against you?

~~***~~

Your world is sometimes turned upside down. It is up to you to tune in your mind to the mind of Christ. That way, you keep your part of the world turned right-side up, and you are righteous before God.

~~***~~

If Jesus had not honestly faced God in the garden, Caiaphas in the Temple, Pilate representing Rome, and the cross on Calvary, we wouldn't have Easter to celebrate!

~~***~~

Sin is complete self-interest. You are a sinner when you trust entirely in yourself and turn away from God. Sin means separation from God: That separation becomes permanent when someone dies in sin. The greatest thanksgiving for a Christian is for the opportunity to live eternally with God because of Christ's gift of His life.

~~***~~

It can be useful to go into a room and imagine Jesus standing or sitting there, watching you - loving you, encouraging you, and guiding you. It is part of trying to make a conscious place for Jesus in your every waking moment.

~~***~~

When you hear the statement, "As you sow, so shall you reap," you are hearing both judgment and promise. God calls upon you to bear fruit with the gifts God has given you.

~~***~~

It is said that a manager is one who gets things done right, while a leader is one who gets the right things done. The church needs both leaders and managers. What is your role?

~~***~~

If we hook up a camera to a timer to record one image each minute of a flower about to bloom, and we play it back at the regular speed, we see that flower truly burst into bloom. It also takes time for development of friendships, love, and sunsets. They take time to be fulfilled.

~~***~~

By God's grace, His forgiveness and redemption continue. By God's grace, you have been called to this place at this time. By God's grace, Jesus and you belong to one another. God's grace is indeed sufficient!

~~***~~

Don't be afraid to say, "God only knows." People will respect genuine humility when it is coupled with confidence. All that God does God does well, but sometimes you cannot see where God is leading you until you share in the completion of God's plans.

~~***~~

Speak less than you pray. No fully functional Christian ever got in ultimate trouble when they spoke after doing their spiritual homework. Serenity comes with completed prayer.

~~***~~

Be honorable. Honor breeds trust - the glue that holds Christian endeavors together.

~~***~~

Every Christian endeavor has a life of its own, but it is connected to the singular life of Christ and His Church. The fruits of the spirit each have their flavor, but all fruits of the spirit come from the same True Vine.

~~***~~

There is righteousness in quality as well as quality in righteousness. Half hearted, half finished, half full efforts do not honor the King of Kings.

~~***~~

Do everything with Christian love. Diplomacy and gentle but firm witness are appreciated by critics as well as by friends. Loving kindness is the lubricant for God's creation.

~~***~~

Deflecting praise for you, to give God the glory is never a wasted effort. Critics as well as friends in a Christian community find it easier to work for God than to work for you.

~~***~~

A fully functional Christian knows when to surrender totally: at the beginning! Are you willing to surrender control to Jesus? Will you do what it takes to be blessed?

~~***~~

Keeping the Sabbath holy enriches your relationship with God, and can contribute to greater intimacy with Our Savior.

~~***~~

Are your motives centered on the good you are doing for yourself or on the good you are doing for others - seeking your own joy or seeking others' joy? "Do unto others as you would have others do unto you."

~~***~~

When it comes to congregational singing, God doesn't care if you can carry a tune accurately. God is pleased when you enthusiastically and honestly express your praise and your love with a song. Accuracy and musicianship do not matter nearly as much as "gusto." Do you sing with GUSTO?

~~***~~

It is a lot easier to tell God what we want than to hear and act on what God is saying to us. Are you spending your time dreaming the impossible dreams of the future? Are you spending your time living in the rosy past? Are you doing the faith work of the present?

~~***~~

The Apostle Paul pointed out the importance of balance between being and doing. Faith without works is dead, but our works should reflect our faith. You begin by being faithful. A Christian is a "be-er" first, and then a "do-er!"

~~***~~

It is very important for you to know not only that you can do all things through Christ, who strengthens you, but also important you are "In Christ" and a "new creation."

~~***~~

What about the gold, frankincense, and myrrh of today? You can still give glory to God and honor the Savior sent by God to pitch His tent among ours. You can honor Jesus rather than simply honor his teachings. You can live a life of disciplined obedience to the God who loves us. You can still give of yourself and give what you value to God. You can still follow the path of the wise men, who gave in order to honor God. How much of yourself can you surrender to God?

~~***~~

Life's longest journey is usually between your head and your heart. As you get older and (hopefully) wiser, you will make the journey more often. Just because you make the journey frequently, however, does not mean that the journey gets any easier!

~~***~~

Jesus often withdrew to pray in order to be sure He was in tune with God's will. When you open your eyes after praying, it is important to remember that Jesus sees through your eyes, just as He works through your hands. When you are aware of Jesus seeing things through your eyes, you begin to see things as He does.

~~***~~

www.ingramcontent.com/pod-product-compliance
Lightning Source LLC
Chambersburg PA
CBHW061454040426
42450CB00007B/1358